THE SE7EN S's

TO

GETTING ANY WOMAN

THE SE7EN S's

To Getting Any Woman

Copyedited by Tia Ross, www.tiarosseditor.com Printed in the United States of America

ISBN: 979-8-218-18322-6

For information about permission to reproduce selections from this book, please contact Rod Warner at Rodwarnerauthor@gmail.com or (214) 241-9229.

THE SE7EN S's

TO

GETTING ANY WOMAN

Rod Warner

CONTENTS

PURPOSE

Early childhood experiences significantly impact a person's identity, perceptions, behavior, and how we navigate our adult life. Throughout my career as a professional mental health therapist, I've witnessed an increasing number of men suffering from the same adverse effects of childhood that I did. This observation motivated me to take a deeper look at the issue, convey the cause and impact, and offer an answer to clients' many challenges. I chose to pursue an education in psychology to learn more about the brain and the hows and whys of our behaviors. I learned that the mind is the gatekeeper of our progression, regression, or stagnation.

Having personally overcome self-esteem issues and negative environmental influences, I counsel other men and equip them with scientific and practical applications to address self-doubt, low self-esteem, and insecurities stemming from adverse childhood experiences. I've noticed an increase in male clients who have displayed problems with social habits disrupting their encounters with women with whom they want to develop a relationship. By creating a nonjudgmental atmosphere and being transparent with clients regarding my relationship woes, men I've encountered in practice feel safe being vulnerable and asking questions that other men and I have kept secret for years: How do I get a super-bad woman? Am I good enough to get a super-hot woman? Why would any woman want to talk to me? Do I have what it takes? However, the most important question at the root of all the prior questions is, "How do I address and overcome my insecurities?"

When men fail to address our insecurities, we tend to overcompensate in other areas of our lives. This suggests that we employ strategic tactics to prevent others from seeing our insecurities.

Things we use to deflect negative attention from our insecurities give us a sort of temporary confidence. Unfortunately, the key issue with temporary confidence is that it always leaves us.

My intention in writing this book is to share with men the language of women. Therefore, *Se7en S's to Getting Any Woman* answers men's questions and focuses on helping men exude confidence to attract women, while guiding them to develop into robust and intuitive mates.

SELF-ESTEEM

Self-esteem is the most critical construct for men in adopting social behavior when interacting with women. When a man has a positive self-image and confidence in his abilities and qualities, it communicates to a woman that he is reliable and trustworthy. Trust is a must in any healthy relationship.

One of my first meetings with someone with exceptional swag occurred on a summer day at the American Airlines Center in Dallas, Texas, just before Beyoncé was to perform. My good friend, Big Rick, had access to the hospitality suite backstage. I tagged along with Big Rick backstage and, to my surprise, he introduced me to influential rap artist and mogul Jay-Z, one of the greatest celebrities at the time. I couldn't believe my luck to be hanging out with these cool New Yorkers. I was impressed with how Jay-Z made direct eye contact with me whenever I asked a question or made a statement, irrespective of the subject. The charismatic way he responded to jokes was characteristically smooth with laughter and not overbearing. His laughter had the right balance to it.

Jay-Z shared a story about a mega superstar he wanted to meet. However, this mega superstar declined the invitation to meet him. Years later, after Jay-Z married Beyoncé, this same mega superstar then wanted to meet Jay-Z. He quickly turned him down. This had me puzzled and baffled.

"Why didn't you want to meet with him?" I asked.

Jay-Z confidently looked at me and said, "Because you don't treat people like that. Always treat people like people because we're all humans."

The way he spoke those words, the extraordinary level of confidence and reassurance he exuded, was indescribable. Later, we headed to the area where Beyoncé was performing. It was mesmerizing to see Jay-Z approach the arena. He walked with outstanding confidence like he owned the damn place. He intentionally spoke to and greeted everyone in his path. I thought, *Wow! How cool is he?* As the night went on, Jay-Z himself poured me Ace of Spades champagne. The swag on this guy was incredible. Through his conversation and my observations, I saw firsthand an authentic, real-life example of swag from, arguably, the G.O.A.T., Jay-Z.

S-1 SWAG

Since its inception and inclusion in the English dictionary, the meaning of the term "swag" has changed. The connotation used here first appeared in the twenty-first century and is widely used in hip-hop and sporting communities. It has been used multiple times by rap artists such as Lil Wayne, T.I., Kanye West, and Jay-Z. This word is used to describe someone who is smooth and has a badass aura. For the sake of this book, I define swag as the intersection of sexiness and coolness. This energizing combo instills a degree of confidence you wouldn't believe. It has been proven by research and relationship experts that women find confidence to be a desirable trait in men.

A group of women were asked on a digital platform to explain why they found confidence attractive. Their responses revealed that they believe confidence will transfer into more positive interactions with men, with one stating, "It's harder for me to like you if you don't even like you." What I am saying to men is believing in yourself and knowing your worth reassures a woman that you will see and appreciate the value in her.

Display Confidence:

- Walk with purpose.

- Adopt good posture. It communicates selfassurance.

- Become knowledgeable on discussion topics or say, "Let me get back to you on that", or "Let me research that further."

- Read and respond appropriately to social cues and settings.

- Make eye contact. It establishes credibility and exudes confidence.

- Don't let mistakes define you. Learn from them and move on.

- Be an independent thinker. It's OK not to go with the majority.

- Be assertive when sharing your thoughts and feelings.

- Keep an open mind. Others' views may differ from yours.

- Speak to everyone and be polite to any person you meet, from the valet to the vice president.

- Show interest in others. Ask people questions about themselves.

SPOKEN WORD

According to Dr. John Gottman, a clinical psychologist and founder of the Gottman Institute, a couple's communication pattern can often predict how successful a relationship will be. It allows individuals to share their thoughts, feelings, and needs and learn things about others.

Dallas Carter High School, which I attended, was one of the most popular high schools in not only Dallas, but also in the entire state of Texas in the late 1980s. Carter High was well-known for its football team, marching band, and attractive girls.

I was sitting in my sophomore English classroom when I saw a girl enter the class. The literature teacher read Keats' poem, "Ode to a Nightingale," aloud and asked questions. I found it difficult to concentrate on my lesson because my thoughts were preoccupied with the most gorgeous girl I had ever seen. I'll call her Alicia. She was of African American descent, with unique eye color that made her stand out even more. I had never known an African American with hazel eyes. Her eyes seemed to hypnotize me when she looked at me, and I found her features utterly captivating.

One day, I somehow mustered up the courage and asked her for her digits, a.k.a. phone number. Mission accomplished, correct? No.

I thought asking for her number would be nervewracking, but the real problem ensued after making the first move. I did not expect the torturous and awkward silence on the phone. Perhaps this was normal initially, as we were just getting to know each other. Unfortunately, this continued for the first, thirty-second, and even forty-second phone calls. The silence was still the same. I knew I was pretty good at initiating conversation, but I missed learning to keep the conversation afloat. The girl I was mesmerized by and anxious to meet was now making excuses to get off the phone every time. To be honest, I couldn't blame her. I neglected to engage her in conversation. So, there I was, sitting in my room after each call, asking myself, "Why is this so hard?" I would've given anything for someone to teach me about the art of segueing in communication with a woman.

S-2 SEGUE

It is normal to have an occasional lull in conversation. Like the pregnant pauses in the conversation between Alicia and me in high school, many of you may find it challenging to keep the conversation moving forward with women. It can seem awkward as you reach for something to fill the void. Fortunately, there are ways that you can segue to pique and keep a woman's interest. Professional assistance is sometimes required and seeing a therapist can help you create good communication patterns, enhance verbal and nonverbal strategies, and increase your overall ability to practice talking more successfully. Learning how and when to segue is a valuable skill that can help you transition seamlessly between topics of conversation. Segueing in conversation is comparable to listening to music on a loop or in an uninterrupted playlist. It sets a continuous vibe, establishes mood, and maintains a conversation flow that engages women by acknowledging their input to help you learn things you have in common. Women appreciate your undivided attention as it assures them they are a priority. They enjoy spending time with men who share their interests. Shared interests are a great starting point for building relationships and aiding an organic conversational flow.

Carry the conversation:

- Acknowledge the other person's input.

- Be an active listener.

- Paraphrase what the other person said and build upon it.

- Ask questions that allow you to learn about her.

- Be prepared to answer questions she may have about you.

- Proactively create a list of topics for discussion.

- Don't be afraid to change the subject if needed.

- Use humor or a tasteful joke.

- Intrigue her with mental and verbal foreplay.

- Seek couple's therapy to address communication inefficacies.

- Become an excellent storyteller.

SIGNALS

Smiling stimulates the brain to produce a chemical reaction that causes you to feel happier. A genuine smile is beneficial to your health and self-esteem, and people are naturally drawn to those who are happy. I grew up in Oak Cliff, a low-income neighborhood of Dallas, Texas. Both of my parents had a high school education and were blue-collar workers. Because of the financial status of most families in our neighborhood, access to certain services was not possible, such as orthodontics. My misaligned teeth made me feel insecure. I matriculated through high school and enrolled in Prairie View A&M with the same crooked, jagged teeth. I was physically fit and drew the attention of female students. However, I was reluctant to smile because I was afraid people would notice my teeth, which were one of my biggest insecurities.

I recall interacting with a group of girls and later overhearing one of them say, "He's really cute. He would be even cuter if his teeth were straight." Overhearing what she said and how she said it crushed me. At that moment, my biggest insecurity was exposed. I didn't smile very much as there was nothing I could do to change the appearance of my teeth then.

Hearing what she said kept replaying in my head for years and made me avoid specific social interactions with women. I began to wear a more severe countenance, making me appear less inviting and approachable. Eventually, I received corrective treatment for my misaligned teeth. Since then, I've never shied away from smiling.

Smiling made me appear more welcoming and, therefore, caused women to feel more comfortable around me. Your smile is often the first and most memorable feature people have of you.

S-3 SMILE

Personal hygiene or upkeep is critical to the success of your dating life. Oral hygiene is one of the essential hygiene behaviors. According to a Match.com survey, 71 percent of women indicated straight, white teeth and a beautiful smile were the most significant features. Conversely, 80 percent said they would not go on a second date with someone if they had bad breath on the first date.

Smiling signifies happiness, confidence, trustworthiness, and approval. It improves our mood and helps our bodies produce cortisol and endorphins, which offer various health benefits. It makes us feel good and can also have the same positive impact on our mates. According to sociologist, Dr. Jess Carbino, "Smiles make you more dateable." When a man smiles at a woman, she receives it as warm and inviting, affirming that she is worthy of your time and attention. Moreover, women are attracted to men with a sense of humor. Engaging women through humor can inspire social bonding by increasing relatability. Making a woman smile/laugh is a fun way to get closer to her.

Lighten up:

- Watch comedy or romantic comedy movies.

- Go on a date to a comedy club.

- Charm her with the right balance of wit.

- Create a level of playfulness to show her your fun and "not so serious" personality traits.

- Find subtle ways to make her smile/laugh (appropriate jokes/riddles).

- Tell her funny stories about you.

- Smile. It's sure to make her smile back.

SAVVINESS

Being knowledgeable, experienced, and well-informed are positive qualities that can be attractive to many people, including women. These traits indicate a person is intelligent, curious, and dedicated to self-improvement, which can appeal to potential partners.

As a child, I held a negative perception of my level of intelligence. I didn't believe I was brilliant because in school, "smartness" was measured by a student's grades. I was told that getting good grades suggest you are smarter. I received poor grades, and it caused me to form a poor opinion of myself. As I became more knowledgeable and gained more exposure to different settings, people, and opportunities, I realized I didn't lack intelligence. Still, the tool utilized (grades) was an invalid means of assessment. I have always been an intrinsically motivated person. Seeing the sacrifices my parents made to provide for us and the financial hardships of those in my community, I knew early in life that I wanted something different. Continuing my education had a significant impact on my life trajectory. I entered college with the self-perception that I wasn't brilliant, but my determination and motivation would prove that theory false. I believe determination and motivation to succeed can be powerful tools to help overcome any self-perception that you may have about your intelligence. Intelligence is defined as the ability to acquire and apply knowledge and skills. Well, I did this with ease. My confidence grew, and so did the influx of women who found intelligence to be one of the most attractive qualities a man could possess. Intelligence quotient (IQ) is incredibly sexy to a woman, and a smart man should continue to learn, grow, and evolve to appear more attractive to the opposite sex.

S-4 SMARTS

Women generally like to have fun. However, they value insight/knowledge over just having a good time. They believe having an intelligent partner can be appealing because it can provide stimulating conversation, shared interests and goals, and a sense of security. There's a word for this attraction, and it is called sapiosexuality. This relatively new term is defined as one who is more attracted to an individual's mind. People who identify as sapiosexual may find that they are particularly drawn to people who are knowledgeable, curious, and good at problem-solving. They may consider these qualities more important than physical appearance or social status when looking for a partner. The Wisconsin Longitudinal Study data followed around 10,000 men and women and discovered that a woman's physical attractiveness predicted her husband's intellect. The study's results suggest that intelligence is vital to a woman when choosing a mate. A woman may specifically seek a partner who is slightly more intelligent than she is, and she may leverage her physical attractiveness to acquire a more intelligent husband. Sapiosexual women are intrigued with learning new or unfamiliar things. As men, we should remain astute on various matters by researching to become familiar so we can speak intelligently about the topic of discussion. There is a thin line between confidence and arrogance. Be sure that you know what to say, how to say it, and when or when not to say it so that you don't come across as an offensive "know it all." As my godfather, Dr. Walter "Doc" Sutton, advised me,

"Learn more so that people will never look down on you and keep learning so that you will not look down on anyone." Women admire intelligence and consideration for others.

Intellectual ideas:

- Challenge your partner's thinking by engaging her in topics that are new to her.

- Communicate clearly when conversing with her.

- Continue to learn new things, including self-discovery, and share new findings with her.

- Participate in shared interests (book study, art exhibits, etc.).

- Remain abreast of current events.

- Discuss details of each other's careers/ambitions.

- Make plans to travel abroad or to historical sites.

- Be an independent thinker.

- Be confident, yet humble.

SALIENT SCENTS

The scent of a man is one of the most apparent or crucial elements that attract women. It can generate an unforgettable memory. My fraternity, Kappa Alpha Psi, Inc., was holding its 2015 national conference in Houston, Texas. This was no ordinary event, it was the Nupes' All-White Affair, the most significant event hosted by Kappa Alpha Psi, Inc. to raise awareness and proceeds that benefit various community organizations. As I walked through the crowd, I bumped into Kim C., an old friend I hadn't seen in years. Reminiscent of old times, we hugged each other, and she immediately noticed and commented on the fragrance I was wearing.

"You smell amazing. What is that you're wearing?"

I replied, "I'm wearing Creed Imperial."

This chance encounter sparked a conversation centered around how I smelled. She was smitten by the scent and stated that it was unlike anything she had ever smelled. I politely thanked her for the compliment but was intrigued to learn what made her so fond of the fragrance. She shared with me that it smelled exquisite. We exchanged pleasantries and chatted for a few seconds before heading back to the event.

Nearly a decade later, I ran into Kim at a local grocery store. As we ventured down memory lane to that event, I was astonished that out of all things, Kim still remembered the smell of that fragrance. This incident confirmed that a scent I wore aroused a woman's sense of smell; that same pleasant fragrance attracted a woman and led me to initiate a conversation with her, leaving a lasting impression on her. Many women are drawn to a man who smells good. Investing in the right fragrance can yield favorable results in the dating pool.

S-5 SMELL

There is no denying the power of smell. *Pheromones* are substances that can operate like hormones outside the body of the person who secretes them, influencing the behaviors of others who receive them. Pheromones can be detected through the sense of smell, and scientists have found a correlation between how a man smells and how strongly a woman is attracted to him. In fact, a man's smell is one of the top three factors that turn women on. To achieve this effect, most major fragrance companies contain pheromones. A study conducted in 2014 revealed that women could distinguish at least one million distinct odors. A man's hygiene can tell a woman a lot about him and his attention to detail. Even without designer fragrances, men must maintain a certain level of hygiene to attract women, like clean hair/beard, teeth, showering, and deodorant.

Often, it is not what we are wearing but whether we are wearing it confidently. NFL Hall of Famer Deion Sanders once charismatically said to an audience, "I don't even use cologne. Somebody asked me, 'What is it that you're wearing?' I said, 'Confidence.'" The smell is part of the chemosensory system and affects a part of the brain that affects emotions, memory, and creativity, and when dealing with women, you'll have to utilize all three. Investing in scents that appeal to women can help men increase their attractiveness.

Recommended repertoire:

Research has proven that scents such as sandalwood, lavender, honey, vanilla, peppermint, pastries, coffee, and cinnamon awaken and stimulate a woman's scent palette.

Colognes

Scents (Calming and Arousing)

- Sauvage (Dior) (sandalwood)

- Creed (Aventus) (lavender)

- Tom Ford (Noir) (honey)

- Chanel (Bleu) (vanilla)

- Baccarat Rouge 540 (peppermint)

- LeLabo 33 (pastries)

- Thallium (coffee)

- Oud Touch (cinnamon)

To learn more about the art of selecting the best fragrances, follow perfume and cologne connoisseur Glenn Davis @MrCologne76 on Instagram.

Hygiene/Housekeeping

- Beard shampoo/moisturizer
- Certain Dri Prescription-Strength Antiperspirant
- Ball deodorant and ball toner
- Lotions with cocoa butter

Clinical

- Baby oil gel
- Bedtime fragrance
- Downy Infusion for fresh-smelling sheets and pillowcases
- Fresh-smelling bath towels

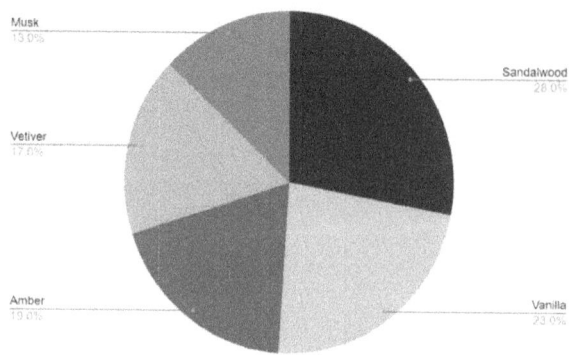

SHARP-DRESSED MAN

Song by ZZ Top

Clean shirt, new shoes
And I don't know where I am goin' to
Silk suit, black tie (black tie)
I don't need a reason why

They come runnin' just as fast as they can 'Cause
every girl crazy 'bout a sharp-dressed man

My alma mater, Dallas Carter High School, had a large student population and was featured in ESPN's *30 for 30* documentary due to incidents surrounding its impressive football record. Along with football, Carter High was also known as a student fashion mecca. Each Friday, everyone wore their best outfit, typically designer-labeled.

The focus on fashion was so intense that students ridiculed those who couldn't wear the latest trends.

I wanted to transfer to a different school to avoid being the target of jokes and humiliation. Meanwhile, my twin brother had a natural affinity for style, easily matching and coordinating his ensembles. My attempts to imitate my brother's style were hit or miss. Style seemed to attract girls, and my lack of it meant I was frequently ignored. I would continue to make the same fashion faux pas, and impede my dating life throughout college.

After college graduation, I set out to spruce up my wardrobe. I studied fashion news and trends, subscribed to fashion editorials, and began following celebrities whose style I admired, like P. Diddy, David Beckham, and the late Regis Philbin. As my social circle expanded, I met others who would be just as influential in my style evolution, such as well-dressed and meticulous spinal surgeon, Dr. Michael Rimlawi of Dallas, and Jay Bradley, an impeccably dressed real estate guru from Houston whose unique style incorporates custom hats. Both men receive lots of attention and compliments because of their sense of style. Their fashion sense indicates they value individuality and are willing to make the extra effort to stand out from the crowd. Affiliation with these two men and learning from their fashion savviness enhanced my clothing style and, ultimately, my confidence.

S-6 STYLE

Dandy, dressy, dapper, fly, and fresh are terms used for style. Style can be defined as a manner of doing something. It's how individuals express themselves through static choices such as accessories, hairstyles, and apparel selection and coordination. The phrase, "Love at first sight" creates a mental image of who and what one visually beholds. There is an immediate attraction to an individual based on their aesthetical appearance or behavior (way of carrying oneself). Style is essential to attracting a woman because it is the initial thing that catches her attention. Style can make a positive first impression and communicate confidence and self-care.

A man's style speaks volumes. It can tell his taste, personality, profession or status, and values. It can also show how much he values his appearance and the effort he is willing to put into grooming. It can be indicative of your drive and ambition. This applies even to the shoes a man wears. Some women may place great importance on a man's shoes and use them to judge his overall style, taste, and attention to detail. They may take this as an indicator of his personality, taste, and hygiene. Studies have shown that 64 percent of women judge a man by his shoes.

This assertion is further supported by Gabriela Cora, MD, a psychiatrist and leadership consultant in Miami, Florida. Dr. Cora states, "Your persona needs to exude your accomplishments without uttering a word. This impeccable look needs to be obvious, from well-cut hair on your head to polished shoes that align with the rest of your image."

A stylish man communicates a bold sense of fashion and confidence. How one presents themselves can indicate that they have a sense of self-awareness and take pride in their appearance. This can be seen as a sign of confidence. Fashion and confidence are a winning combination when presenting yourself to a woman. A man's investment in himself communicates to women that he will do the same for her. I suppose there is some truth in ZZ's Top's song: "Every girl crazy 'bout a sharp-dressed man."

Your fashion arsenal should include the following:

Accessories

- Scarf

- Watch

- Bracelet

- Belt

- Handkerchief/pocket square

- Lapel pin

- Necktie/bowtie

- Gloves

- Hat

- Coat/jacket

- Eyewear (glasses/sunglasses)

Shoe Basics

1. Brown loafer

Stylish summertime/comfortable/slide-on, penny loafer, oval penny driving shoe i.e.,

2. Sneaker

Casual/canvas or leather material/outdoor and indoor activities, i.e., Capri Sneakers, Vans, and New Republic

3. Monk Strap Distinctive/versatile/traditional/trendy, i.e., Williams' Single Monk Strap by Cole Hann, Fletcher Double Monk Strap by Johnson & Murphy, Hoyt Monk Strap by Beckett Simonon

4. Chelsea Boot

Sexy/stylish/versatile may be worn with jeans, slacks, chino, suit, or sports jacket, i.e., duke, suede, and chuck

SCRIPTURE

"All Scripture is breathed out by God and profitable for teaching, for reproof, for correction, and for training in righteousness, that the man of God may be complete, equipped for every good work." – 2 Timothy 3:16–17

I volunteered at the Chocolate Mint Foundation's Annual Christmas "Candyland" in late December. Gospel Grammy Award-winning artist Kirk Franklin was in attendance. While I was there, Kirk shared with attendees how God had changed his life in an impactful way. He shared with us how he communicates with God daily through prayer. It was a bit different from what I had thought it would be. It wasn't a very formal prayer or way of praying. Rather, Kirk stated, "Keep in mind that

God is your daddy, and you should speak with him as if He is your daddy."

This struck a chord with me as I compared talking to my heavenly father with talking to my earthly father. The same principles would apply. I would speak to him daily, being respectful, grateful, and obedient, and maintain a healthy fear for his position. Putting it in perspective like this made my relationship with God more appealing and attainable. Kirk shared several other helpful tips about having a relationship with our Father, God. Following this encounter, I took Kirk's advice and began praying and reading the Bible more intentionally. I prayed and read the Bible every morning. As I read and learned more about the stories of the Bible, I became more fascinated and intrigued. This was more insightful than anything I had learned from sitting and listening to One day, I was talking to a friend and a group of her girlfriends about a particular story in the Bible where a donkey spoke words (Numbers 22:21-39). To my surprise, the expressions on their faces signaled how engaged they were with the message. The following day, my friend phoned me to let me know that several of the girls talked about how intrigued they were by my level of biblical knowledge. I wondered what made sharing a Bible story so impactful. My friend explained, "It's extremely attractive when a man takes time to study God's word. It exudes confidence and knowledge and exhibits a spiritual foundation that makes women feel safe." I then realized how powerful a man's spirituality can be in guiding us in the right direction and to a suitable mate. A man who studies his faith may be perceived as wise, thoughtful, and grounded, which can be attractive.

S-7 SPIRITUALITY

Spirituality encompasses the idea that there is an intangible and eternal part of us, referred to as "spirit." We must feed our spirit just as we recognize and care for our physical bodies. This can be accomplished through mindfulness practice, prayer, and seeking guidance and wisdom. My experience of spirituality is rooted in the biblical context. Some scriptures support why spirituality positively impacts relationships between men and women. For example, the Bible instructs husbands to love their wives as Christ loves the church. Though the passage was written in connection with marriage, it can also be used to teach respect outside of marriage. Women who desire God are inclined to be attracted to men who are connected to Him. A man's connection to the source [God] can communicate to a woman that his priorities are correctly aligned and that he can care for and provide for her.

Additionally, a man's connection to God may be seen as a sign of humility, compassion, and openmindedness. It may also indicate that he is committed to living according to a specific set of values and moral principles. According to another text, God gave man sovereignty over the land. Subsequently, the woman was made for the man. A man spiritually attuned and guided by God is seen by some as more attractive, credible, and capable of leading a woman and household.

A man guided by God may be seen as compassionate, empathetic, and kind. He may also be seen as open-minded, humble, and driven by a strong moral compass. Higher levels of spirituality have also been linked to increased compassion, strengthened relationships, and improved self-esteem, which has been associated with heightened levels of serotonin and oxytocin, also known as "love hormones." Thus, a man's spirituality can increase his chances of attracting a mate. A strong spiritual connection and a sense of purpose can make them more attractive to potential partners, indicating they are grounded, centered, and at peace with themselves.

Spirituality has individual implications as well. It can help fulfil your purpose. Devoting time to self-discovery and purpose equips you to become a better man. The Greek philosopher Socrates said, "Know thyself." Learning who you genuinely are creates self-awareness and can be a huge confidence booster. Your confidence level is attractive to a woman because it conveys that she can rely on you to be resourceful in providing safety and care.

Women have historically been attracted to men with power. What better way to attain power than to connect directly to the power source (God) through prayer? "For Thine is the kingdom, the power, and the glory," (Matthew 6:13). Simply put, women love a man who is connected to a source higher than themselves. It imparts humility and diminishes ego.

Enhance spiritual connection by:

- Prayer - fosters connectedness and reduces feelings of isolation, fear, and anxiety
- Journaling - helps you get to know yourself and identify thoughts and feelings

- Self-reflection - learn about yourself, your purpose, and areas you need to work on

- Yoga - improves mental acuity and improves mood

- Meditation - increases mindfulness and prevents excessive worry

- Diet and exercise - increases serotonin (mood-boosting hormone)

- Physical touch - consensual touch increases oxytocin (mood-boosting hormone)

- Time in nature - improves mental health and cognition

- Volunteer - builds connectedness, empathy, generosity, and gratitude

- Support/social network - makes connections and reduces isolation and depression

SANCTUARY

A place of refuge and protection, solace, and peace.

My curiosity grew around the idea of mate selection. I was curious about why people in relationships selected one another. I would speak with multiple people and ask each of them the same question, "What was it about him or her that made you decide this is the one?" Answers varied from being in love, beauty, physique, friendly smile, sense of humor, religious affiliation, etc.

The most thought-provoking response I received was from a woman who said she chose to be in a relationship because the man made her feel safe. As she shared more, she revealed that past traumas and instability aligned with her priorities and the traits she sought in a mate. Ultimately, she desired a man who could protect her—a man she could rely on to act in her best interests. She wanted to feel safe—safe enough to share her innermost secrets, safe enough to be vulnerable, safe enough to open her heart and love her man without limits. I would advise men to write down this password and use it when trying to gain access to her heart. The password is S-A-F-E.

BONUS – SAFE

When a man protects and provides for his partner in a relationship, he establishes a level of dependability that fosters trust. Trust is vital for making a woman feel safe. Charles Green, the founder of Trusted Advisor Associates, created the Trust Equation Model to help understand the components of trust. His equation describes trust as:

$$\text{Credibility x Reliability x Intimacy} \div \text{Self-interest} = \text{Trustworthiness}$$

This is possible if she feels you're knowledgeable, trustworthy, and concerned about her well-being. The extra "S" (Safe) is extremely powerful because its absence eliminates all the other Se7en S's. When a woman feels safe, this decreases her levels of anxiety. Feeling safe in a relationship allows partners to be open and vulnerable enough to be themselves without the risk of intentional harm from each other. For a woman, having a sense of both physical and emotional safety is a requirement for a successful, healthy relationship. When a woman doesn't feel safe, she may become guarded to avoid the feeling of hurt. If she continues to feel unsafe, her anxiety may cause her to go into fight, flight, or freeze mode.

Ways to create safety:

1. Spend intentional time with her

This is also a preferred love language, "Quality Time." You're making a conscious decision to see her and make time for her. It's been said that "time is money," and the investment of your time communicates to her that you value her. Your effort shows her that you care enough to make her a priority.

2. L.U.V. her

The acronym's meaning is not synonymous with "love." Instead, it means to Listen to, Understand, and Validate her.

L-Listen: Effective listening means you're attentive to her and what matters to her.

It builds trust, allowing her to become more comfortable being open with you.

U-Understand: Take the time to ensure that your interpretation accurately reflects what she is communicating. This can be done by giving her your undivided attention, asking clarifying questions, and repeating what she said to ensure you're on the same page. This makes you more relatable, as you can identify with what she is saying.

V-Validate: Validation affirms to a woman that her feelings matter. You can do this by trying to see things from her perspective. This is not to say that you must agree. Instead, it says, "I hear you,

I see you, and I understand where you're coming from."

3. Recognize her

When a man recognizes a woman, it establishes her identity in the relationship. This acknowledgment will let her know you appreciate and value her contributions. In short, receiving your recognition creates a sense of security for her.

4. Accept her

Acceptance is an unspoken agreement to engage in a relationship with the understanding that neither party is flawless. This is when you have decided upon the things you can and cannot live with. Acceptance creates a sense of belonging and reassurance that she is in a safe, nonjudgmental relationship. Moreover, it says you want her, flaws and all. The Serenity Prayer is a reminder of the power of acceptance.

"God, grant me the serenity to accept the things I cannot change, the courage to change the things I can, and the wisdom to know the difference." – Reinhold Niebuhr, 1943

5. Be reliable

Knowing that she can depend on you leads to a pattern of predictability that she can trust. A woman feels protected when her man has proven to be trustworthy and takes care of her emotional and physical well-being. Make sure your words align with your actions.

6. Make her feel wanted

Nothing is more appealing to a woman than making her feel wanted or desired. Being wanted/desired is a more profound yearning for someone that consumes your daily thoughts. Being with someone you "want" is a selfless display of their importance to you. It says I am not choosing you for self-gratification. Instead, I want you to just be you. Women love to hear that you want, long for, and crave them. Making her feel wanted can make her feel safe and have a lasting impact on her.

7. Be consistent and stable

Consistency and stability are dynamic combinations that can contribute to positive long-term effects in a relationship. Consistency is the heartbeat of any task you're trying to accomplish. When you are intentional in your behavior/actions consistently over some time, it can make a woman feel safe and secure. Equally important, the presence of stability is a must in a relationship. Remaining consistent and unyielding shows your commitment to being there for her, which can alleviate any abandonment worries she may have had. Your stability reflects your capacity to rationalize, remain calm, and avoid overreacting.

She will feel safe knowing you control a situation instead of being controlled by it.

8. Fight for her

Fighting for her can be defined as perseverance. There are no perfect relationships because there are no perfect people. Disagreements are inevitable. Fighting for her means you are committed and will not give up at the first sign of trouble. It's been said that anything worth having is worth fighting for. During your disagreement, remember that words mean everything to a woman. So, be cautious and aware of your words. Don't say things you don't mean. Keep in mind that the human brain does not record dates and times. However, it does keep a record of how an experience made one feel. Show her that you will fight for her and with her. Note, if you have to fight "her" for "her," you should consider individual and couple therapy as this means an intrinsic issue needs to be addressed.

9. Pray for her

Interceding for her is a surefire way to maintain a successful relationship. When she knows God is the top priority in your life, she will have confidence in your ability to lead and care for her. Openly praying for her in her presence makes her feel connected and safe. As a child I saw hanging wall plaques in most homes read, "A family that prays together stays together." Couples can adopt this practice and pray together. Praying for her is an endearing way of letting her know how much you care for her. In my experience, a woman loves and respects a man who knows how to pray. Remain mindful that she needs your prayers, and you need the practice to remain connected to the "source" [God].

10. Articulation

Gentlemen, have you ever felt this way before?

"I know what I'm trying to say, but it's not coming out the way I'm trying to say it."

In the words of Erykah Badu, "What good do your words do if they can't understand you?"

In relationships, not understanding how to express oneself can be troublesome. Words matter, and women hold us accountable for what we say. A man's first goal should be to communicate clearly. Articulation is crucial to helping a woman gain clarity and understanding. However, it's not merely enough to be clear in speaking. It is equally important to ensure that what is said is understood. If a woman has clarity without understanding, this will confuse her.

Lack of clarity plus lack of understanding equals confusion. A woman's confusion can lead to distrust, which causes her to feel unsafe. Clarity explains the "What," and understanding explains the "Why." Providing clarity will answer questions like: What are we doing? What are you talking about? And what am I supposed to do? Getting an understanding will provide answers to other questions, such as: Why are we always talking about this? Why are we doing this? Why aren't we moving forward?

A man who understands how to express himself verbally can communicate his thoughts and feelings. For a woman, this indicates she can feel safe with him.

You are now well-informed and equipped to use the principles shared here in *Se7en S's to Getting Any*

Woman. Not only will you be able to get her, but you will know how to treat her with dignity and respect to ensure longevity in your relationship.